Falling between Worlds

Catalogue of video art 2016-2020

Tess Baxter : Tizzy Canucci

Dane Stone
Publishing

www.tessbaxter.com | tizzycanucci.com

Published by Dane Stone Publishing
Ulverston, Cumbria LA12 8LB
www.dane-stone.co.uk

ISBN: 9780-955-374944

Typeset in Gentium and Lato by Tess Baxter,
as Dane Stone Publishing.

Printed by Ex Why Zed. www.exwhyzed.co.uk

Introduction

Second Life is a three dimensional virtual world, and an online space. It is not a game designed by a studio, and instead it is distinctive for being a user created space, where people often invite and encourage others to share and rework what they create. It is also inherently ephemeral, and so this book records my experiences of the places I worked within, and recognises the creativity of the people involved in making them.

I see my artwork as 'video art', coming out of, rather than being just within, Second Life. I mix material from Second Life with shared content from across the internet, reflecting how the 'digital' and 'analogue' are joined. I find the alternative label of 'machinima', a name that grew out of the early days of video gaming, too restrictive, as it is now tied to commercial interests and pure game play. Indeed, my video art connects more strongly with animation, feminist experimental film, new queer cinema, and the legacy of imaginative expressionism of Méliès than commercial story telling from Hollywood or its equivalent.

This catalogue lists the video art I made during the period 2016-2020. The first, Our Music of the Spheres, which was the first selected for a festival, the Supernova digital animation festival in Denver, in 2016. The catalogue ends with the 2020 selection, out of isolation came forth light.

Within my video art, I also use public domain and Creative Commons licensed material from the internet. There is no requirement to give credit for public domain or Second Life material, but for me, ethically, I should. I have tried to be generous, but I apologise for the limitations and for omissions.

This was also broadly the period when I was working on a PhD in contemporary art at Lancaster University. As practice-led research, theory and practice live together, rather than one dominating the other. It affirmed my view that everything in 'the digital' comes from outside of it, and is connected to other forms of art, literature and history.

As a development of this I took still images from my video art into printmaking, from light on screen to ink on paper, so cycling ideas and visuals back to the space outside of 'the digital'. The results of the printmaking are not included in this catalogue, but can be found at www.tessbaxter.com.

Tess Baxter

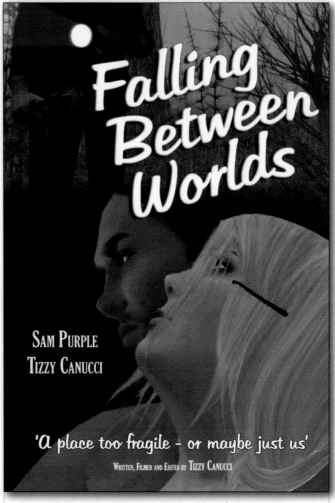

The catalogue title, *Falling Between Worlds*, refers to a video artwork made in 2017. On the one hand, it alludes to the way people in Second Life talk about going back to 'real life'. On the other, it addresses real or actual life, of history and of racial segregation in the United States during the mid-twentieth century, and politics today (page 10).

There are other virtual worlds, such as OpenSim, but none have the maturity of Second Life. Second Life is a trademark of Linden Research, Inc., trading as Linden Lab.

Content Layout

Table content
Date
Vimeo link
Exhibitions
Description
Blog post
Location
Artist
Music

The 'poster' for the video is shown at the top of each page, with some stills at the bottom.

Date is when it was published on Vimeo, and works are listed in date order.

Vimeo link takes you to the work.

Exhibitions lists the film festivals, art exhibitions and academic conferences where it was shown in full, sometimes as an installation in a gallery.

Description gives general information on how the work came about, links to other works, and references to theory.

I wrote about some of my videos in my *blog* and these include thoughts about Second Life, technology, and the social and political situations and influences. Some of this came from, or went into, the PhD, but the writing was aimed at a Second Life, or more general, audience.

Location was where 'filming' was done in Second Life. These are sometimes referred to as a 'sim' or 'region'. I have included the names of those involved in creating or running them, but was sometimes ambiguous or I did not make a record. Some places still exist, but many have now gone.

The last few categories, most often *artist* and *music*, name the people most directly involved in creating the work that I used and reworked, some from inside and some from outside of Second Life.

Following the catalogue of video art there is a section of *Additional links*, which includes further information on material that was referred to briefly in the *Description*.

The Digital Pilgrims (page 13)

Our Music of the Spheres

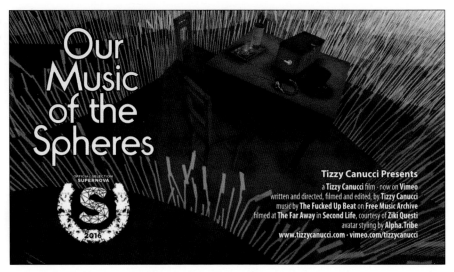

Date	10 August 2016
Vimeo link	https://vimeo.com/tizzycanucci/musicspheres
Exhibitions	Selected for *Supernova Digital Animation Film Festival 2016*, Denver, 24 September 2016.
Description	A film poem combining words, images and music. As always, the process is cyclical - an idea, some filming, a search for music, then back to the idea again. But with words also involved, there was also an interaction between the images, the music and words that developed through the process. I had already decided on the opening visual of the radio, and this coincided wonderfully with the public domain voice in *Junction City Fields*. I was unable to quite tell what was being said, but I could pick up parts of it and a sense of meaning. This led to me to think more about the railroad not simply being a rusted junction but also a metaphor for other divisions.
Blog post	https://tizzycanucci.com/2016/09/25/of-music-spheres-and-emotions/
Location	The Far Away, maintained by Ziki Questi: https://maps.secondlife.com/secondlife/Dreamworld%20North/198/152/22
Participant	Sadie Gee
Music	The Fucked Up Beat: *Junction City Fields*

The Pillars

The Pillars

A film by Tizzy Canucci

The Pillars: Four Moments of Contemplation
An installation by Oberon Onmura

Split Screen Installation Space in Second Life
Curator, Dividni Shostakovich

Filmed and edited by Tizzy Canucci
August 2016

Date	25 August 2016
Vimeo link	https://vimeo.com/tizzycanucci/thepillars
Description	A documentary film of an installation: 'The Pillars: Four Moments of Contemplation' by Oberon Onmura. The sim owner and curator Dividni Shostakovich said; 'It is a forest of mountain pillars inhabited by four bots, each in his own soundscape. And then, something flickers... Oberon is known for his minimalist yet evocative style, sometimes highly scripted, and other times (such as this) more metaphoric.' The audio was a sound recording made at each quarter of the installation. Made with an older computer set up that really struggled with the graphics, it was working with what 'happened' as deliberate actions were difficult.
Location	*Split Screen Installation Space*, curator Dividni Shostakovich: https://maps.secondlife.com/secondlife/Amra/73/14/24
Artist	Oberon Onmura

Symphony for a Lost King

Symphony for a Lost King

A Tizzy Canucci film.
Performance by SaveMe Oh at the Josef K Galleria dell'Arte in
Second Life, 30 September 2016.
Music by DJs Morlita Quan, Yadleen SL & Echo Starship.
Additional music by Zero V.
Filmed and edited by Tizzy Canucci.
© Tizzy Canucci 2016, CC BY-NC-SA

Date	7 October 2016
Vimeo link	https://vimeo.com/tizzycanucci/symphonylostking
Description	In this performance, SaveMe Oh was overlaying visuals in a more complex and interactive manner than I had seen previously. I did not feel that video techniques I had used previously, mostly blending and overlaying, did it justice aesthetically.
	The DJs were were mixing music into distinctive work, which I thought was more interesting as audio tracks, rather than finding Creative Commons music. I felt I could claim 'fair use' for its blending and academic use, but that is too contestable and I avoided doing it again.
	However, the clip that formed the third section stood out as an unedited two minute 'movement'. The tempo was adagio, which led me to think about adopting a symphonic four movement structure. This thought, influenced and informed by historical processes, was a critical innovation in practice, as a reworking of the conceptual divide between analogue and digital. At nine minutes this video was longer than previous ones.
Blog post	https://tizzycanucci.com/2016/10/09/making-symphony-lost-king/
Location	*Josef K Galleria dell'Arte*
Artists	SaveMe Oh performance, with Morlita Quan, Yadleen SL and Echo Starship playing music live in Second Life
Music	Zero V: *Bell Zouki*

1. Adagietto

2. Lento

3. Adagio

4. Meditativo poi vivace

There is No Cure for Curiosity

Date	4 November 2016
Vimeo link	https://vimeo.com/tizzycanucci/nocureforcuriosity
Exhibition	*Interface*, an art exhibition of 23 artists by neo:artists, held at neo:gallery23, The Market Place, Bolton, 31 March - 20 May 2018. Shown continuously with *Future City*. Continuous showing in a shipping container with *Future City* at *Mobile Utopia: Art and Experiments*, an exhibition of the work of 13 international artists curated by Jen Southern, Emma Rose and Linda O Keeffe. Part of the *Mobile Utopia: Pasts, Presents, Futures* conference held at Lancaster University, 2-5 November 2017.
Description	*Insilico* is a long established sim, but was facing closure. Distinctive in appearance, it reflected the idea of life in the future based in a science fiction influenced setting. There was also a history of controversy and some dubious practices, admitted to by Skills Hak in her blog. And yet that reflects the development of the internet, with partially regulated spaces that both have interesting experimental and novel ideas and take unfair advantage of their users. My video also reflected my view on how the idea of dystopia was changing. In particular, Brexit and the election of President Trump in the US were connected to people experienced in exploiting the internet for political ends. Science fiction as a literary form has also a history of responding to the present to create a view of the future. Audio was more important than previously, by overlaying and fusing ambient sound, music and multiple spoken elements. It is not comprehensible all at the same time deliberately.
Blog posts	https://tizzycanucci.com/2016/11/11/curiosity-dystopia-insilico/ https://tizzycanucci.com/2018/03/29/interface-at-neogallery23-bolton/
Location	*Insilico*: https://maps.secondlife.com/secondlife/INSILICO/190/182/3602
Creator	Skills Hak
Music	Laura Sheeran: *Rain Song*; MindsEye: *Stellar*
Web page	Insilico website; Skills Hak blog

The Very Discrete is Now Visible

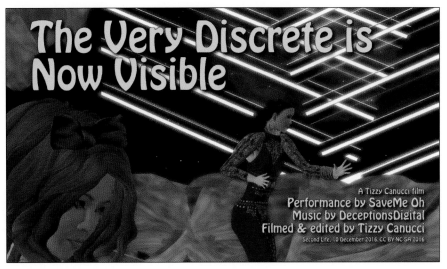

Date	13 December 2017
Vimeo link	https://vimeo.com/tizzycanucci/verydiscretenowvisible
Description	The visuals are overlaid throughout, and silhouettes, shadows and avatars emerge and dissolve, sliding from foreground to background through the visuals by SaveMe Oh.
	This was the first time I used the lumakey effect in Lightworks to anything like this extent. It was important in achieving visually mixed effects that would add a further quality to the visual effects that were present in the performance, as a form of montage or collage.
Blog post	https://tizzycanucci.com/2017/01/17/whats-in-a-frame/
Artists	SaveMe Oh performance, with DeceptionsDigital playing music live in Second Life

Edward Thomas

Edward Thomas
A film by Tizzy Canucci

Poems: 'The Bridge', 'How At Once', 'In Memoriam (Easter 1915)' by Edward Thomas. 'Edward Thomas' by Tizzy Canucci. © Tizzy Canucci 2017. Creative Commons BY-NC-SA

Date	24 January 2017
Vimeo link	https://vimeo.com/tizzycanucci/edwardthomas
Description	A work based on the poetry of Edward Thomas, with an introduction by myself. Edward Thomas was born in London in 1878 to a mostly Welsh family. A foremost literary critic of his day, he turned to poetry in 1914 with the encouragement of Robert Frost. He could have avoided enlisting to the army, but still did so in 1915. Although labelled as a war poet, rather than war being literal, violent or vivid, it was a shady unsettling presence on the edges of his poetry. He died in the Battle of Arras in 1917.
	I discovered his poetry in 'O' level English in 1975, and he has been a constant and an inspiration as a writer ever since. The video starts with my writing, reflecting this. I had not previously thought about working literature together with virtual world imagery. Again, sound is critical, but here each voiced element is tied to visuals in a continuous single flow.
Blog post	https://tizzycanucci.com/2017/02/06/speak-softly-let-your-voice-carry/ https://tizzycanucci.com/2016/09/10/from-supernova-to-edward-thomas/
Location	*Jane Austen's English Countryside* at LEA8 by Tigre Milena and Armon Aeon; *Costa Blanco*: https://maps.secondlife.com/secondlife/Costa%20Blanco/29/216/29; *Skybeam Sandbox*: http://maps.secondlife.com/secondlife/SkyBeam/71/71/38
Literature	Edward Thomas: 'The Bridge', 'How At Once' & 'In Memoriam (Easter 1915)'; my ow personal writing about my experience of his poetry
Audio/ Images	Schnabel ST aka Timo Tschentscher: *Audio of Common Swift, Apus apus*; Personal audio recordings of swifts; pau.artigas: *Falciot #2* (image of swift)

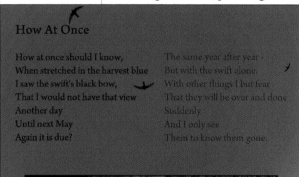

Zed &
Two Ohs

Date	10 February 2017
Vimeo link	https://vimeo.com/tizzycanucci/zandtwoohs
Description	Several years before this video, Peter Greenaway made a call within Second Life to abandon the frame, with the aim of inspiring new approaches in machinima making. It was a significant idea used in this video.
	Bryn Oh and SaveMe Oh have an acrimonious relationship in Second Life, and this was a way of setting their work against or within each other. They have a different attitude to what art should be. Bryn creates narratives in the structures she builds, and visitors are directed to follow a story. SaveMe makes art performances using objects that her avatar 'wears', very much in the moment, and wants to prompt immediate responses, often through controversy.
	SaveMe Oh's performance was recorded first. My avatar is seated in front of Bryn Oh's building and is 'wearing' a green-screen just behind her, between the building and the stairs and projector. The overlaying of the two video images was done in editing.
Blog post	https://tizzycanucci.com/2017/01/17/whats-in-a-frame/
Location	*Hand*, by Bryn Oh: https://maps.secondlife.com/secondlife/Immersiva/15/99/31
Artists	SaveMe Oh performance with DeceptionsDigital playing music live in Second Life

Falling Between Worlds

Date	17 March 2017
Vimeo link	https://vimeo.com/tizzycanucci/fallingbetweenworlds
Description	The Story of Cathy and Sam, caught between two worlds in 1950s America; a fictionalised story drawing on actual events in a racially divided nation. The story resonated in the political climate of 2017, not least with how Donald Trump was elected as US President and early political moves, as discussed in the blog post. In 2020, with a surge in Black Lives Matter over police racial discrimination, its relevance became even more apparent.
	I am rarely drawn to telling stories as I am more interested in visual expression and believe narrative will emerge. This was different, the idea growing from the rainy setting of the sim, and a passing comment about rain during the inauguration ceremony of Trump. Connections with Todd Haynes's *Far From Heaven* followed initial production, as I recognised commonalities in the story-line. I also adopted some of the Douglas Sirk imagery that influenced Haynes.
Blog post	https://tizzycanucci.com/2017/04/01/falling-between-worlds/
Location	*One Caress*, by Squonk Levenque and Miuccia Klaar: https://maps.secondlife.com/secondlife/Beck/97/143/1992
Music	Fabrizio Paterlini: *Veloma*; Mattie Delaney: *Tallahatchie River Blues*
Audio	White House: *The Inauguration of the 45th President of the United States*; Robert Wimer: *1 Hour Thunderstorm*

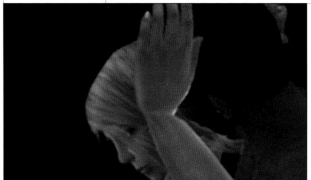

white
on
indigo

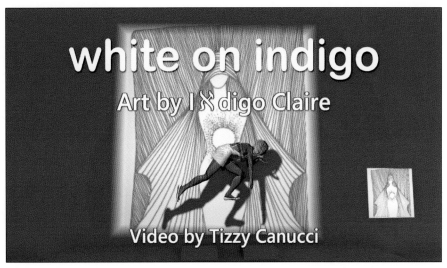

Date	24 April 2017
Vimeo link	https://vimeo.com/tizzycanucci/whiteonindigo
Description	A piece of art, and some music, an avatar and a few poses.
	The video explores Second Life in a literal way. People make psychological choices about the poses they want to give their avatars, to give them a more human feel. In a virtual world, they can be read as natural. However, showing them in a video exposes their repetitive mechanical actions, almost like a Victorian automaton.
	In the video, the difference between avatar and art is reduced to pose and skin colour. Unlike the previous video, *Falling Between Worlds*, there is no narrative, and instead returns to the idea of the visual. It can be perceived as either a short video or an extended photograph.
Blog post	https://tizzycanucci.com/2017/05/03/white-on-indigo/
Location	*The Glue House*
Artist	Indigo Claire
Music	Musick's Recreation: JS Bach, *Suite in G Minor, BWV 995: VII. Gigue*

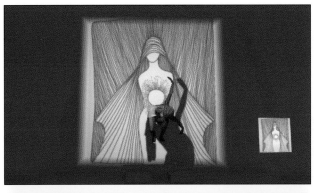

Swirl Eight

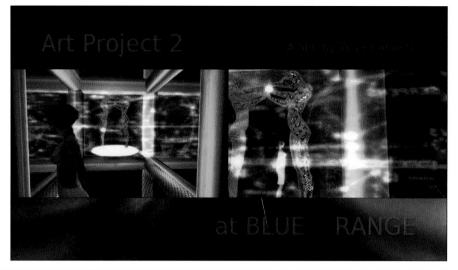

Date	14 May 2017
Vimeo link	https://vimeo.com/tizzycanucci/swirleight
Description	There are numerous galleries in Second Life, and most art shows that are hosted in them have an opening event involving music and dance.
	This video captured the light, colour and people of an art show opening. This is once again a study of how avatars behave in a virtual world. Most animations are now made using 'motion capture', a computer recording of the motions of a live human action. It is a reflection of idealised interpretations of human behaviour, that become also quite mechanical by the way they are limited to a series of loops.
Location	*Blue Orange*, a place organised by In Inaka: https://maps.secondlife.com/secondlife/Empire%20State%20Island/213/28/1435
Artists	Theda Thammas, Cica Ghost, Rebeca Bashly, Jarla Capalini, Gitu Aura, NicoleX Moonwall, In Inaka, Igor Ballyhoo
Music	Wildlight: *Twirl Me*

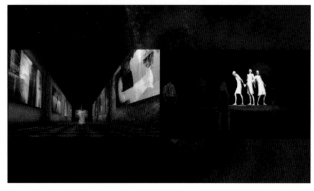

The Digital Pilgrims

Date	31 July 2017
Vimeo link	https://vimeo.com/tizzycanucci/thedigitalpilgrims
Exhibitions	Selected as semi-finalist, *FilmArte Festival*, Madrid, 18 October 2019. Selected for *Supernova Digital Animation Film Festival 2017*, Denver, 23 September 2017 (Below, top right). Basis of selection for interview in *WomenCinemakers Special Edition*, March 2018.
Description	A fusion of the medieval world that Geoffrey Chaucer was writing about in *The Canterbury Tales* and today's digital world. The reading of the 'Prologue to the Canterbury Tales' in Middle English by Kristen Hughes was important in providing context.
	Each character is introduced in turn, with a letter but no explanation. They are sometimes similar to their medieval predecessors, sometimes a modern equivalent, and sometimes a blend of the two. In the final section, the characters are name with two lines of text, the wording reflecting those characteristics across time. These are fully listed in the blog. The video was a way of exploring how the digital/ analogue divide is more about ways of looking and a complete revolutionary change.
Blog post	https://tizzycanucci.com/2017/08/11/the-digital-pilgrims-rediscovery-and-reinvention/
Location	*Furillen City*, by Serene Footman; *Foxcity*
Music/ Images	Circus Marcus: *Levantarán el vuelo*; Scans of C19-C20 books: British Library
Literature/ Audio	Geoffrey Chaucer *The Canterbury Tales*; both Librarius & Project Gutenberg: Chaucer's 'Prologue to the Canterbury Tales', lines 1-18, spoken by Kristen Hughes; Librevox

Future City

Date	17 August 2017
Vimeo link	https://vimeo.com/tizzycanucci/futurecity
Exhibitions	Selected for *Foresight Film Festival N°4: Top Down - Vision reaches city*, Urania Berlin, September 2019 (below, top left). Shown continuously in a bus during the Visual Research Network Conference, *Creative Image: Ways of Seeing, Representing and Reshaping Reality*, Manchester University, 26-27 September 2018 (below, bottom left). Shown continuously with *No Cure for Curiosity*, at *Interface*, an art exhibition in Bolton (2018), and at *Mobile Utopia: Pasts, Presents, Futures Conference* at Lancaster University (2017): see *There is No Cure for Curiosity* for details.
Description	The differing views of cities of the future taken in archive footage and virtual worlds are set against each other in this video. Cica Ghost's *Future* in Second Life is overlaid by a film from the FDR archive on the future of the American city made in 1939. The background music and voices in the film are remixed with music by contemporary musicians, The Fucked Up Beat, who themselves used samples of older sound material. This work continues previous practices of mixing material and diminishing and negating the analogue/ digital distinction. In his book, *Mixed Realism*, Timothy J Welsh claims that the virtual and the real are not opposed, but fold into each other, and so the fictional is joined to the material and the cultural. Discrepancies and gaps are important in making us aware of how the virtual mediates the real, and as film mediates the past. We do not have, and cannot have, direct experience of one without some of the other.
Blog posts	https://tizzycanucci.com/2017/08/17/mixed-realism/ https://tizzycanucci.com/2018/03/29/interface-at-neogallery23-bolton/
Location	*Future*, by Cica Ghost
Music	The Fucked Up Beat: *Hunted in the Capitalist Steppes/ Zero History*
Archive film	*The City* (1939)

Fish

Date	31 August 2017
Vimeo link	https://vimeo.com/tizzycanucci/fish
Description	A (more or less) abstract piece based on the visuals of SaveMe Oh and the music of Deceptions Digital, and purely exploring the visual aesthetic. The original clip was filmed in February 2017 in one take, moving through SaveMe Oh's performance area in three dimensional space. Editing includes post-processing and typographic elements.
Artists	SaveMe Oh performance, with DeceptionsDigital playing music live in Second Life

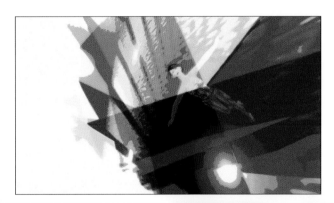

Breaking Ice: a 70 Year Story

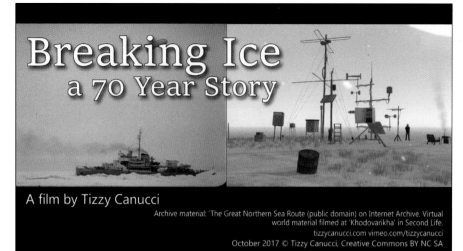

Date	4 October 2017
Vimeo link	https://vimeo.com/tizzycanucci/breakingice
Description	Archive film meets virtual world, from mechanical reproduction to digital arts. An audiovisual essay exploring how the view of the Arctic has similarities and differences across both media and time. The archive film is *The Great Northern Sea Route*. Made in the USSR in 1947, it relates the endeavour of reopening the sea route through the Arctic as part of the five year plan immediately after the Second World War. The virtual world video was collected at a Second Life reconstruction of Khodovarikha, an actual location on the Barents Sea coast. Both show a fascination in different lands and people, set in different contexts. Adrian Martin and Cristina Álvarez López argue that film is a visual medium that words cannot completely summarise, and so there is an academic strength in using the visual. Word based analysis assumes greater clarity, as if there is no ambiguity of meaning in the written word. In contrast, visual analysis recognises that viewers interpret what they see, when the role of the academic is to present frameworks of their own understanding. This is not the only video where I work with this idea; in several I do this in different ways at different levels. Virtual worlds, and the videos that can be made in them, have less inherent visual information, which reduces their ability to 'speak', yet I wanted the two visual forms to be in dialogue. In response to the critique by Martin and Álvarez López, the text I added does not interpret the visual difference between the film and the video, but adds an additional layer, of information about the place that is more about the actual world today.
Location	*Khodovarikha*, by Serene Footman and Jade Koltai: https://maps.secondlife.com/secondlife/Porter%20Islands/78/181/22
Archive film	*The Great Northern Sea Route* (1947)

The Safe Shipment of Small Cargo

Date	17 January 2018, revised July 2020
Vimeo link	https://vimeo.com/tizzycanucci/safeshipment
Description	The exhibition of artworks in containers by Marina Münter was first displayed at *Berg at Nordan Art* in September 2017, then *Art in the Park* in June 2020, before being homed at *The G.B.T.H. Project* in July 2020. This video art combines the artwork with *Outgoing Cargo!*, an archive film made in the 1950s for the National Association of Manufacturers in the United States. It promoted American capitalism, and introduced the viewer to 'a steel container called a cargo van', as a new innovation for shipping. Coincidentally, during November 2017 two pieces of my own video art, *There is No Cure for Curiosity* and *Future City*, were shown in a shipping container as part of the *Mobile Utopia* conference at Lancaster University. The 2018 version included *Mobile Utopia* video, which was never quite satisfactory, and which was replaced in 2020.
Blog post	https://tizzycanucci.com/2018/01/20/new-art-in-old-containers/
Location	*Berg at Nordan Art*, run by Kate Bergdorf; *Art in the Park,* run by Vally Lavender: http://maps.secondlife.com/secondlife/Lavender/141/53/21; *The G.B.T.H. Project,* run by Marina Münter: https://maps.secondlife.com/secondlife/the%20GBTH%20project/52/220/37
Artist	Marina Münter
Archive film	*Industry on Parade: Outgoing Cargo* (1950s)

Art in
Two Acts

Date	2 February 2018
Vimeo link	https://vimeo.com/tizzycanucci/artintwoacts
Description	Two art exhibitions. Both were interesting builds or arrangements, demonstrating different examples of how art is made and presented in Second Life. In many ways they emulate 'real world' spaces and galleries, the difference being in the expressive qualities of the virtual artwork in space and time.
	The reason behind doing them as two 'Acts' was to establish an artistic connection, which was more about an experience and feel rather than a definition.
	Act I: *Sapiens, Gem's land of Fractals* by Gem Preiz at *LE29*.
	Act II: *Dreamer's Feelings* by Magda Schmidtzau and Ciottolina Xue at *Trésor de l'Art*.
Location	*LE29; Trésor de l'Art*
Artists	Gem Preiz; Magda Schmidtzau and Ciottolina Xue
Music	Krackatoa: *The big out there*

Here is
your
Sandwich,
you
Spoiled
Thing

Date	3 March 2018
Vimeo link	https://vimeo.com/tizzycanucci/yoursandwich
Description	The music and one of the performances was from 22 February 2018, with additional visual material recorded at a performance on 15 November 2017. The key technique was overlaying visually, and using lumakey in Lightworks for editing and visual dynamics.
Location	*Cats Circus*, by Cat Boucher
Artists	SaveMe Oh performance, with Yadleen SL playing music live in Second Life

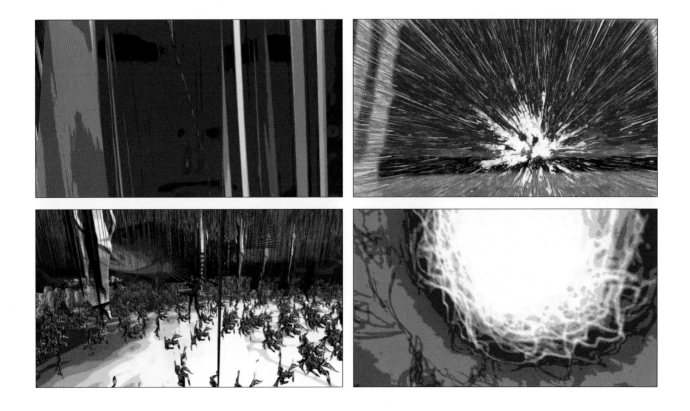

In A Bowl

Date	12 March 2018
Vimeo link	https://vimeo.com/tizzycanucci/inabowl
Description	Decomposing images of SaveMe Oh's performance, with music by A Limb. The audio incorporates one of A Limb's most successful and popular sound pieces. The visual is a continual rotation around the A Limb avatar, which increases in speed over time through video editing. The disrupted appearance was from using a stylised simulation effect for Lightworks video editing software. This emulates in digitally created video the technical problems and faults inherent with the repeated use of analogue video-tape.
Location	*Circus at Gaudi Park,* at *LEA1,* built by Barlok Barbosa, Cat Boucher, Daddio Dow, Eifachfilm Vacirca and Alex von Kottwitz, dragonmaster and scripts by Bavid Dailey: https://maps.secondlife.com/secondlife/LEA1/140/118/51
Artists	SaveMe Oh performance, with A Limb playing music live in Second Life

Innominate

Date	22 April 2018
Vimeo link	https://vimeo.com/tizzycanucci/innominate
Exhibitions	Selected for *Supernova Digital Animation Film Festival 2018*, Denver, 22 September 2018. Shown as part of an exhibition, *Tell me a story*, at CRUgaleria, Porto, Portugal, 4 May–28 July 2019, which brought together the work of about 26 artists who had produced work at *Delicatessen*.
Description	Meilo Minotaur greeted visitors with 'whoever tells a tale, adds a point', a Portuguese saying, inviting them to make a story from what had been placed there. I used a visual stream, a textual flow of consciousness, sounds, and bassoons. I resisted telling a story, instead creating a descriptive list written as a flow, in the knowledge that the visuals would inevitably be read and interpreted by the reader as a narrative. The title, Innominate, means 'without a name' or 'not classified' and was a creative choice linked to my locality; Alfred Wainwright called a previously unnamed water in the Lake District 'Innominate Tarn' in one of his guidebooks.
Blog posts	https://tizzycanucci.com/2018/04/23/showing-or-telling/ https://tizzycanucci.com/2018/10/01/sunny-in-denver-for-supernova/ https://tizzycanucci.com/2019/05/15/tell-me-a-story/
Location	*Delicatessen*, by Meilo Minotaur with CapCat Ragu: https://maps.secondlife.com/secondlife/Porto/12/132/21
Music	Grossman, Ewell, Grainger: Robert Rønnes, *Trio for Three Bassoons*
Audio	InspectorJ: *Bird Whistling, Single, Robin*

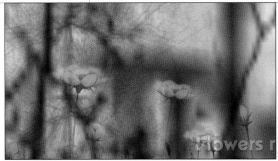

Neither Paris Nor Sweden

Date	20 June 2018
Vimeo link	https://vimeo.com/tizzycanucci/parisnorsweden
Description	The Second Life video of the performance is cut and montaged with a public domain archive film from the Prelinger Archive, made 104 years earlier. It connects my own interests in life - virtual worlds now and swing and blues dance in the past.
	The archive film is listed as recording the interior of a Black dance hall with a band and dancers, but the quality of the light has more of an outside feel. The dance steps are not an obvious genre, but social dance often worked with building routine, not just copying it. It has features similar to how balboa, blues and lindy hop are danced today, and the loose hold used by the partners is an interesting feature. The dancers in the final sequence reveal a remarkable level of skill to retain balance and footwork through such fast spins.
	Once again, the video aims to bridge time and events, and see the analogue and digital as a continuity that has commonalities, rather than the newer one just replacing the past.
Location	*VeGeTaL PlaNeT*: https://maps.secondlife.com/secondlife/Oak%20Park/109/194/2
Artists	SaveMe Oh performance, with Morlita Quan playing music live in Second Life
Archive film	*[Gould can 5423.4]* (1914)

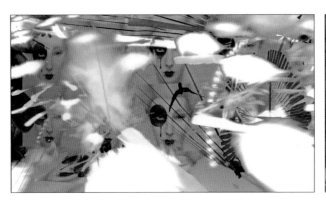

Repeat Hikari

Date	28 July 2018
Vimeo link	https://vimeo.com/tizzycanucci/repeathikari
Exhibitions	Selected for *Supernova Digital Animation Festival 2019*, as one of 15 artists in prestigious 'Competition' program, Denver, 21 September 2019 (below, top right) NWCDTP Postgraduate Conference, *Digital Humanities, Human Technologies*: continuous showing in foyer of Salford University at MediaCity, 10-11 October 2018 (below, bottom right).
Description	In Amelie Marcoud's installation stacked televisions repeat images in endless loops. This video works, reworks and repeats her theme, with images that are endlessly repeating, with a deliberate intention of making that looping repetition obvious. The looping images emphasise the looped nature of animation in Second Life, something equally true for trees as the 'human' avatar. Avatar animations appear 'natural' in-world when part-watched but are mechanical, like Victorian automatons, when viewed attentively at a distance. Stoppages occur as animations repeat, when returning from an end point to the start.
Blog post	https://tizzycanucci.com/2018/08/01/art-looping-repeating/
Location	*The G.B.T.H. Project* by Marina Münter and Megan Prumier: https://maps.secondlife.com/secondlife/Starry%20Night/204/231/3186
Artist	Amelie Marcoud
Music	Little Glass Men: *Apache Force*

Missing Kake Broek

Date	21 November 2018
Vimeo link	https://vimeo.com/tizzycanucci/misskakebroek
Description	Video made at an event on 10 November 2018 for the opening of an exhibition of Kake Broek's (possibly final) artistic statements, following his ban by Linden Lab. Three floors of his distinctive images were shown in the gallery, and the event was held on the roof. On 31 May 2018, Kake posted on Flickr a letter from Linden Lab which they stated he had been banned 'for severe or repeated violations of the Second Life Terms and Conditions... or related policy'. The main offence was 'misrepresentation as a Linden', with Kake's satirical artistic statements presumably being taken at face value and overstepping a mark. Appeals by residents, and further arguments by Kake, failed to change Linden Lab's view and position. The gallery was deleted from Second Life shortly after.
Blog post	https://tizzycanucci.com/2018/06/04/cleaning-up-the-streets/
Location	*Amsterdam*: https://maps.secondlife.com/secondlife/Amsterdam/15/151/25
Artists	Kake Broek; SaveMe Oh performance, music by Option Y, and DJs Elwood and d-oo-b
Music	The Conquering Light Of Flora And Fauna: *Easy Christian Kill*

OK, OK

Date	7 December 2018
Vimeo link	https://vimeo.com/tizzycanucci/ok-ok
Description	A video that works with visuality in Second Life, accompanied by music sampled from the internet. In particular, it uses creative breakdown, where the original is recognisable, but only just, and the pace restricts recognition. It deliberately moves out of spatial realism into blurring aesthetics across time. Visual mixing mostly used the lumakey effect in Lightworks.
Location	*M.A.N.T.I.C.O.R.E.*: https://maps.secondlife.com/secondlife/Aube/213/20/614
Artists	SaveMe Oh performance; Kaia Beattie and Khaz Rotaru, DJs
Music	Nine Inch Nails: *1,000,000*

Deliberare Humanum Est

Date	11 December 2018
Vimeo link	https://vimeo.com/tizzycanucci/deliberare
Description	Marina Münter argues 'Deliberare Humanum Est: Because pretending we're not seeing it is diabolical'. While claiming her work raised more questions than answers, this was her direct response to the recent election of Jair Bolsonaro in Brazil, another man in a lengthening list of democratically elected populist leaders. All claim to stand aside of politics, but only as a 'justification' to deny consensus positions. Far from being apolitical, behind them is a web of connections to unaccountable power cliques willing to suppress dissent and erase differing views.
	The political commitment was the main reason I chose to make a video from this art installation. While some of my earlier work does this - *Our Music of the Spheres*, *There is No Cure for Curiosity* and *Falling Between Worlds* in particular - here it is explicit. It also rejects Jay David Bolter and Diane Gromala's view that digital artists want you to look at the surface, not beyond.
Blog post	https://tizzycanucci.com/2018/12/11/the-art-of-seeing/
Location	*The G.B.T.H. Project*, by Marina Münter: https://maps.secondlife.com/secondlife/Starry%20Night/204/231/3186
Artist	Marina Münter
Music	Madame Rrose Sélavy: *Despacho (Instrumental)*

Waiting Edges

Date	2 March 2019
Vimeo link	https://vimeo.com/tizzycanucci/waitingedges
Description	Made at *Chesapeake Bay*, another atmospheric and visually interesting installation by Serene Footman and Jade Koltai. Once again, it was inspired by and loosely based on an actual place, *Khodavarikha* being the most significant previous one, with *Breaking Ice: a 70 Year Story*.
Location	*Chesapeake Bay*, by Serene Footman and Jade Koltai: https://maps.secondlife.com/secondlife/Epsilon/33/206/21
Music	Blue Dot Sessions: *Uncertain Ground*
Audio	BBC Sound Effects: *Cliff top with seagulls circling overhead*

Sound Living

Date	1 June 2019
Vimeo link	https://vimeo.com/tizzycanucci/soundliving
Description	The music and the place has drawn me back to *Chouchou* regularly since I first arrived in Second Life over ten years ago. It demonstrates the best that virtual worlds can offer - an evocative experience in an artistically created space that generates feel and atmosphere - rather than some suburban planned community and dwelling space.
	The music on *ChouChou* was composed by the creators of the place, juliet Heberle and arabesque Choche, and it is available at https://chouchou.bandcamp.com/. However, I chose different sounds, primarily because the experience of music in a three dimensional virtual world is different from a two dimensional video. As the musicians were not responding to questions from Second Life at that time, getting permission was not a possibility in any case.
Blog post	https://tizzycanucci.com/2019/06/02/sound-living/
Location	*Chouchou* and *Momento Mori*, by juliet Heberle and arabesque Choche: https://maps.secondlife.com/secondlife/Chouchou/180/163/21
Audio	BBC Sound Effects: *Seawash: Distant seawash and gulls (For use at low level)*; Church Bells: *Single bell ringing, Notre Dame, Paris*

Art
Tartaruga

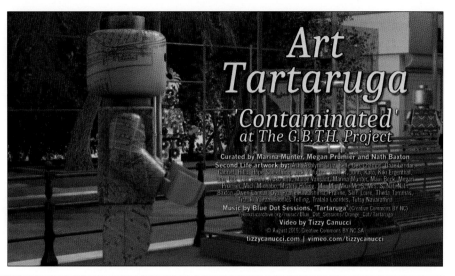

Date	16 August 2019
Vimeo link	https://vimeo.com/tizzycanucci/art-tartaruga
Description	The G.B.T.H. Project hosts some of the most interesting art and exhibitions in Second Life. This was the first edition of *Contaminated*, which opened in January 2019. In terms of video work, working out how to add my own contribution to a static series of artworks took time.
	There were three influences working through it. Firstly, Godley and Creme's music track *Cry* in 1985 was an early exercise in blending images of human faces in video. Secondly, in searching for music I came across 'tartaruga', which fitted in mood. But the name has the colloquial meaning of 'slow person' in Portuguese, so fitted well with the blended still images. Thirdly, images of the artwork, each with the artist's name, were available in Second Life, so I copied, cropped, and overlaid them to highlight and include all the artists involved.
Blog post	https://tizzycanucci.com/2019/08/16/tartaruga/
Location	*The G.B.T.H. Project:* http://maps.secondlife.com/secondlife/the%20GBTH%20project/113/131/42
Artists	Marina Münter, Megan Prumier & Nath Baxton, with 37 other SL artists
Music	Blue Dot Sessions: *Tartaruga*

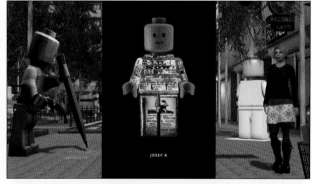

Menuetto
Contained

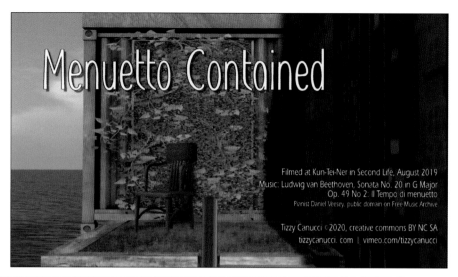

Menuetto Contained

Filmed at Kun-Tei-Ner in Second Life, August 2019
Music: Ludwig van Beethoven, Sonata No. 20 in G Major
Op. 49 No 2: II Tempo di menuetto
Pianist Daniel Veesey, public domain on Free Music Archive

Tizzy Canucci © 2020, creative commons BY NC SA
tizzycanucci.com | vimeo.com/tizzycanucci

Date	30 January 2020
Vimeo link	https://vimeo.com/tizzycanucci/menuetto-contained
Description	Ini Inaka has been long active in art and music in Second Life, setting up *Blue Orange* as a space, and at an exhibition opening there in May 2017, I made *Swirl Eight*.
	Streaming video into Second Life without glitch has been a perpetual problem. Ini was hosting a promising experimental approach at *Blue Orange*, albeit using the deprecated Adobe Flash, which has security issues and will only be supported until the end of 2020. She approached me to make a video, and I used material I had been unable to work with in 2019. Nineteen artist videos were shown, and about seventy people's avatars were present at the event itself, as shown in the image below, top left.
Blog post	https://tizzycanucci.com/2020/01/31/video-in-second-life/
Location	*Kun-Tei-Ner* by Lotus Mastroianni and Fred Hamilton https://maps.secondlife.com/secondlife/Fallen%20Angel/45/186/39
Music	Daniel Veesey: Ludwig van Beethoven, *Sonata No. 20 in G Major, Op. 49 No. 2: II. Tempo di menuetto*

Squares Circles and String

Date	2 April 2020
Vimeo link	https://vimeo.com/tizzycanucci/menuetto-contained
Description	As with *Menuetto Contained*, this came out of an approach from a Second Life resident. I had previously made *Glass and Light Breakwave* from the artwork of Thoth Jantzen (Djehuti-Anpu), in October 2015. Although I always try to reinterpret artwork, I see them as also providing a record; something confirmed by Thoth, as he said he had lost a part of the installation.
	This video was at an event where Thoth Jantzen provided the visual effects, with additional particle effects by Venus Adored. Music at the event was Hardwired, LIVE Electronic Music, and Shade of Loud with Mix Magickby. As always, however, I chose music that was more suited for cutting the visuals, which has a different dynamic from music selected for avatars to dance to at a performance.
Blog post	https://tizzycanucci.com/2020/04/04/squares-circles-and-string/
Location	*Moon Endowment for the Arts:* https://maps.secondlife.com/secondlife/Tropical%20Delight/44/33/3424
Artists	Build by Zara and Thoth Jantzen, visual art by Thoth Jantzen
Music	Andre Jetson: *String Theory*

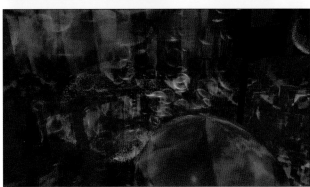

Of
Shui Mo
Virtual

Date	9 April 2020
Vimeo link	https://vimeo.com/tizzycanucci/ofshuimovirtual
Description	Made in response to the exhibition 窗户 Chuānghu (Windows) by FionaFei at the G.B.T.H. Project. As always the mixing of forms of technology was attractive. FionaFei stated in the notecard: "Chuānghu is an architectural installation in the style of ink wash. It is a modern take of today's urban environment, especially crowded areas filled with buildings and structures that are close together. In the meantime, it also provides a type of openness, where all the 'walls' are see-through, acting as windows... It is my hope that visitors will take pictures, where each picture is a piece of art". A space that obviously works with the similarities and different between ink and digital light, as I do with my printmaking, and encourages collaboration at a distance.
Blog post	https://tizzycanucci.com/2020/05/15/art-borrowing-and-science/
Location	*The G.B.T.H. Project:* http://maps.secondlife.com/secondlife/the%20GBTH%20project/219/94/52
Artist	FionaFei
Music	Kevin MacLeod: Erik Satie, *Gymnopedie No 2*

Transmission
is Ten

Date	11 April 2020
Vimeo link	https://vimeo.com/tizzycanucci/transmissionisten
Description	At one level, this was personal, reflecting the amount of time I had spent in this club, most Friday and Saturday late evenings for about four years, and the music and the people. But at another level, it marks the longevity, persistence, and social connection that exists in this virtual world. That a communal space, set up and sustained by a small group of individuals, exists for ten years is notable on the internet.
	Technically the video is imperfect and a compromise. The standard frame rate for video is 30 frames per second. However, as active objects, avatars reduce the frame rate, and it is related to the number present. The viewer can be set to limit the number seen in detail, which keeps the frame rate up, but at the cost of appearances. I set the viewer to sixteen, but the frame rate was still dropping to less than 20fps. Ordinarily I have techniques for limiting the number of active objects on camera to keep the frame rate up, but here it would have defeated the point.
Blog post	https://tizzycanucci.com/2020/04/13/time-spent-together/
Location	*Transmission*: http://maps.secondlife.com/secondlife/Atlantis%20City/214/162/22
Music	The Matt Kurz One: *Wake Up Little Siouxie*

isolation

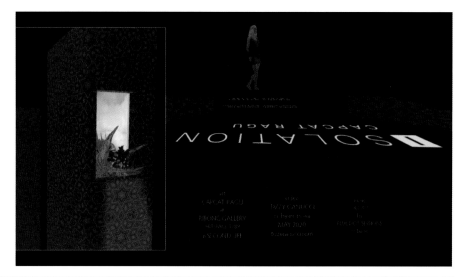

Date	12 May 2020
Vimeo link	https://vimeo.com/tizzycanucci/isolation
Description	*Isolation*, an exhibition by CapCat Ragu, struck me for its clarity and understatement. The most commonly adopted symbolism of Covid-19 were absent; the face mask, and images of a virus that is too small to see except with an electron microscope. Both of those make the human the subject, as if the virus is merely a spectacle. I thought the dark emptiness and the isolated enclosure of an outside world in towers was effective by stepping back from the iconography.
	I used sparse music, included my solitary self standing, and created a period or space of black through which the word 'isolation' slowly fell, was my way of reflecting that sense of distance and odd separation. The subdued narrative, open space, and a lingering zone of nothing have more in common with the animation of Studio Ghibli than film-making.
	I previously worked with CapCat's art in *Innominate*.
Blog post	https://tizzycanucci.com/2020/05/15/art-borrowing-and-science/
Location	*Ribong Gallery (Artspace), Mieum*: http://maps.secondlife.com/secondlife/Mieum/177/23/1790
Music	Blue Dot Sessions: *I Recall*

Flames Tear the Soul

Date	30 May 2020
Vimeo link	https://vimeo.com/tizzycanucci/flamestearthesoul
Description	Made in response to Supernova Digital Animation Festival 'kicker line' for 2020 of 'World on Fire'. It is biographical, connecting Beethoven's *Heiligenstädter Testament* with my own experiences of injury, with the complete collapse of a sense of the future that followed. It included Second Life artwork around both politics and Covid-19, as well as virtual world aesthetics, which ties into C Wright Mills view that 'personal troubles cannot be solved merely as troubles, but must be understood in terms of public issues'. As Beethoven put it, and with which the video finishes: *'Farewell and love each other'*.
Blog post	https://tizzycanucci.com/2020/06/04/flames-tear-the-soul/
Location	*Dathuil Gallery of Art:* http://maps.secondlife.com/secondlife/Floris/181/82/24 *Flossify Gallery:* http://maps.secondlife.com/secondlife/Silvercreek/234/57/23 *Eternal Conflict:* http://maps.secondlife.com/secondlife/Helcaraxe%20Isle/134/129/28 *Cornhub:* http://maps.secondlife.com/secondlife/NORTH%20KOREA/128/128/29
Artists	Marina Munter, SaveMe Oh
Music and Literature	Czech National Symphony Orchestra: Ludwig van Beethoven, *Symphony No. 3 in E Flat Major 'Eroica', Op. 55 - II. Marcia funebre Adagio assai.* Ludwig van Beethoven, *Heiligenstädter Testament*

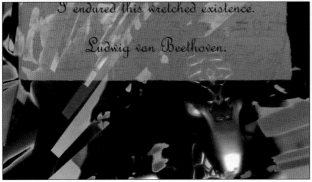

out of isolation came forth light

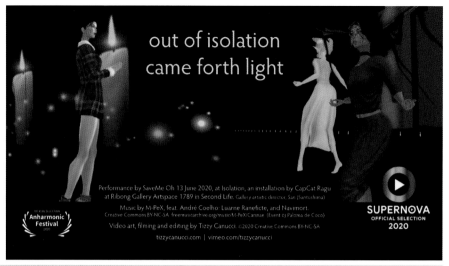

out of isolation
came forth light

Performance by SaveMe Oh 13 June 2020, at Isolation, an installation by CapCat Ragu
at Ribong Gallery Artspace 1789 in Second Life. Gallery artistic director, San (Santoshima)
Music by M-PeX, feat. André Coelho: Luarne Raneficte, and Navimort.
Creative Commons BY-NC-SA. freemusicarchive.org/music/M-PeX/Carinae. (Event of Paloma de Coco)
Video art, filming and editing by Tizzy Canucci. ©2020 Creative Commons BY-NC-SA
tizzycanucci.com | vimeo.com/tizzycanucci

SUPERNOVA
OFFICIAL SELECTION
2020

Date	23 June 2020
Vimeo link	https://vimeo.com/tizzycanucci/cameforthlight
Exhibitions	Selected for Anharmonic Film Festival 2020, and Supernova Digital Animation Festival 2020.
Description	A social event at CapCat Ragu's installation, *Isolation,* where I had previously made a work, with music by a DJ I knew, Paloma de Coco. I hadn't expected SaveMe Oh, but then perhaps no one ever does. CapCat and Paloma are both Portuguese, which influenced the choice of music. SaveMe's performances are very much responsive, performance events rather than being planned beforehand. I like the spontaneous, as it carries the possibility of something good and unexpected - the result of serendipity the bringing together of accident and sagacity with inventiveness, as Sebastian Olma defined it. In turn I have previously reinterpreted her work in ways she has both liked and disliked. However what I brought here was more blending and working with. As she commented on Vimeo: 'We really touch the soul of saudade'; touching souls is not done through routine, but through a feeling and a sense of being in the world.
Blog post	https://tizzycanucci.com/2020/06/27/came-forth-light/
Location	*Ribong Gallery Artspace 1789:* http://maps.secondlife.com/secondlife/Mieum/177/23/1790
Artists	CapCat Ragu, SaveMe Oh
Music	M-PeX, feat. André Coelho: *Luarne Raneficte* and *Navimort*

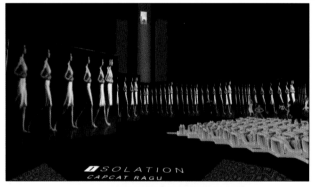

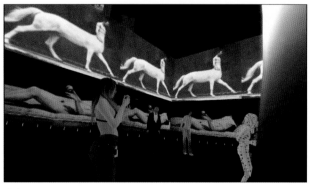

Additional links

Our Music of the Spheres

The Fucked Up Beat (2017) *Junction City Fields*. Free Music Archive. Music online.
  http://freemusicarchive.org/music/The_Fucked_Up_Beat/Insomnie/
  The_Fucked_Up_Beat_-_Insomnie_-_06_Junction_City_Fields.

Supernova (2019) Supernova Digital Motion Art Festival.
  https://filmfreeway.com/Supernova.

Symphony for a Lost King

Zero V (2012) *Bell Zouki*. Free Music Archive. Music online. http://freemusicarchive.org/
  music/Zero_V/Travelling_A_Collection/13_Zero_V_-_Bell_Zouki.

There is No Cure for Curiosity

Hak S (2016) I wanted to post this sooner but i am rather busy... In: *CVNT*. Blog.
  http://skills.tumblr.com/post/141699124267/byeeee.

Insilico (2016) Insilico guidelines: roleplay Info. Wiki.
  http://insilico.wikidot.com/background-info.

MindsEye (2016) *Stellar*. Free Music Archive. Music online.
  http://freemusicarchive.org/music/MindsEye/MindsEye/MindsEye_-_Stellar.

Sheeran L (2013) *Rain Song*. ThisIsOpenMusic! Music online. http://freemusicarchive.org/
  music/Laura_Sheeran/Music_for_the_Deep_Woods/05_Rain_Song.

Edward Thomas

Baxter T (2016) My own recordings of swifts in Kendal, UK.

pau.artigas (2010) *Falciot #2*. photo. https://www.flickr.com/photos/paussus/4560391937.

Schnabel ST (2016) *XC331848 Common Swift (Apus apus)*. xeno-canto. https://www.xeno-
  canto.org/331848. Contributor named as Timo Tschentscher at time of making the
  video.

Thomas E (1979) The Bridge. Online academic archive.
  http://ww1lit.nsms.ox.ac.uk/ww1lit/collections/item/2860.

University of Oxford (n.d.) The Edward Thomas Collection.
  http://ww1lit.nsms.ox.ac.uk/ww1lit/collections/thomas.

Zed & Two Ohs

Harvey C (2010) *Peter Greenaway speaks at 48Hour Film Project Machinima 2010*. Vimeo. Video
  online. https://vimeo.com/groups/8472/videos/15253336.

jayjayzifanwe (2011) Peter Greenaway Interview following review of entries to
  MachinimUWA III: Journeys. In: *The University of Western Australia (UWA) in Second Life*.
  Blog. http://uwainsl.blogspot.com/2011/05/peter-greenaway-interview-
  following.html.

Falling Between Worlds

Delaney M (1930) *Tallahatchie River Blues*. Memphis: Vocalion Records. 78: Music online.
  https://archive.org/details/MattieDelaney-tallahatchieRiverBlues.

Haynes T (2002) *Far from Heaven*. Focus Features. DVD.

Paterlini F (2009) *Veloma*. Clinical Archives. Music online.
  http://freemusicarchive.org/music/Fabrizio_Paterlini/Viandanze_EP/Veloma.

The White House (2017) *The Inauguration of the 45th President of the United States*. The White
  House. Video online. https://www.youtube.com/watch?v=4GNWldTc8VU&t=68s.

Wimer R (2010) *1 hour thunderstorm*. Free Music Archive. Audio online.
  http://archive.org/details/1HourThunderstorm.

white on indigo

Musick's Recreation. Milena Cord-to-Krax (2016) *JS Bach: Gigue (BWV 995)*. Seville: Free
  Music Archive. Music online. http://freemusicarchive.org/music/
  Musicks_Recreation_Milena_Cord-to-Krax/Una_Reverencia_a_Bach/
  Musicks_Recreation_Milena_Cord-to-Krax_-_06_-_Gigue.

Swirl Eight

Wildlight (2013) *Twirl Me*. Jumpsuit Records. Music online.
  http://freemusicarchive.org/music/Wildlight/Hers_Was_As_Thunder/Wildlight_-
  _Hers_Was_As_Thunder_-_01_Twirl_Me_1133.

The Digital Pilgrims

British Library (2007) Chaucer book artwork C19-C20.
https://www.flickr.com/photos/britishlibrary/.

Canucci T (2018) Tizzy Canucci. Interview in WomenCinemakers Special Edition, 30
March, 2018. Magazine article, pp 52-75.
https://issuu.com/women-cine-makers/docs/special.edition/2.

Chaucer G (1997) Geoffrey Chaucer (1342-1400) 'The Canterbury Tales' (in Middle English
and Modern English). http://www.librarius.com/cantales.htm.

Chaucer G (2000) *The Canterbury Tales, and Other Poems*. Purves DL (ed.). Project Gutenberg.
http://www.gutenberg.org/ebooks/2383.

The Digital Pilgrims (cont.)

Circus Marcus (2017) *Levantarán el vuelo (Orchestral Version)*. Free Music Archive. Music
online. http://freemusicarchive.org/music/CIRCUSMARCUS/~/
MasteringBOX_circus_marcus_-_levantan_el_vuelo_birds_-_orchestral.

Circus Marcus (2017) *Levantarán el vuelo (Piano Solo)*. Free Music Archive. Music online.
http://freemusicarchive.org/music/CIRCUSMARCUS/~/
Levantarn_el_vuelo_Piano_Solo.

FilmArte (2019) FilmArte - The Film Festival for Art Films & Films about Art(ists).
http://filmartefestival.com/.

Hughes K (2007) *Prologue to the Canterbury Tales, Lines 1-18*. LibriVox. Music online.
http://archive.org/details/canterbury_prologue_librivox.

Supernova (2019) Supernova Digital Motion Art Festival.
https://filmfreeway.com/Supernova.

Future City

Baxter T (2017) There is No Cure for Curiosity. In: *13 Art Works, 12 Experiments in Mobile
Utopias*. Lancaster: Lancaster University, p. 29.

Baxter T (2018) Future City: video art and the montage of virtualities and realities. In:
Creative Image: Ways of Seeing, Representing and Reshaping Reality, Manchester, 26
September 2018. https://www.visualresearchnetwork.co.uk/vrn-2018.html.

Baxter T and Canucci T (2018) *Conference exhibitions summer 2018*.
https://vimeo.com/295693127/e95952e511.

Canucci T (2017) There is No Cure for Curiosity: Moving between worlds using
machinima. In: *Mobile Utopia: Pasts, Presents, Futures Conference, 2-5 November 2017*,
Lancaster, 2 November 2017. Lancaster University.
http://wp.lancs.ac.uk/t2mc2c/programme-2/.

science2public (2019) Foresight Filmfestival: science meets vision.
https://foresight-filmfestival.de/.

Steiner R and Dyke WV (1939) *The City*. Internet Archive/ FDR Presidential Library/
Prelinger Archive. Video online. https://archive.org/details/0545_City_The.

The Fucked Up Beat (2016) *Hunted in the Capitalist Steppes/ Zero History*. Free Music
Archive. Music online. http://freemusicarchive.org/music/The_Fucked_Up_Beat/
Records_Vanishing_Crop_Circles_and_Occult_Rituals_in_the_Future_Age_of_Paranoia
_by_The_Fucked_Up_Bea/The_Fucked_Up_Beat_-
_Records_Vanishing_Crop_Circles_and_Occult_Rituals_in_the_Future_Age_of_Paranoi
a_-_02_Hunted_in_the_Capitalist_Steppes-_Zero_History.

Welsh TJ (2016) *Mixed Realism: Videogames and the Violence of Fiction*. Minneapolis:
University of Minnesota Press.

Breaking Ice: a 70 Year Story

Frolenko V (1947) *The Great Northern Sea Route*. Internet Archive/ National Archives and
Records Administration. Video online.
http://archive.org/details/gov.archives.arc.44539.

Martin A and Álvarez López C (2017) Writing in Images and Sounds. Online academic
magazine. http://sydneyreviewofbooks.com/writing-in-images-and-sounds/.

The Safe Shipment of Small Cargo

Baxter T (2017) There is No Cure for Curiosity. In: *13 Art Works, 12 Experiments in Mobile
Utopias*. Lancaster: Lancaster University, p. 29.

Bergdorf K (2017) Non-Perishable: An Exhibit by Marina Münter at Berg by Nordan Art –
The Bergdorf Reports. In: *The Bergdorf Reports*. Blog.
https://katebergdorf.wordpress.com/2017/08/31/non-perishable-an-exhibit-by-
marina-munter-at-berg-by-nordan-art/.

National Association of Manufacturers (1950s) *Industry on Parade: Outgoing Cargo, Workhorses of the Harbor, Refresher Course.* Internet Archive/ Prelinger Archive. Video online. http://archive.org/details/IndustryOnPa.

Art in Two Acts

Krackatoa (2015) *The big out there.* Free Music Archive. Music online. http://freemusicarchive.org/music/krackatoa/The_Big_Out_There/Krackatoa_-_The_big_out_there.

Innominate

Grossman A, Ewell T and Grainger B (1984) *Robert Rønnes: Trio for Three Bassoons.* Pandora Records. Music online. http://freemusicarchive.org/music/Grossman_Ewell_Grainger/Bassooniana/Grossman_Ewell_Grainger_-_Bassooniana_-_04_-_Roennes_Trio_for_Three_Bassoons.

InspectorJ (2018) *Bird Whistling, Single, Robin, A.wav.* Freesound. Audio online. https://freesound.org/people/InspectorJ/sounds/416529/.

Supernova (2019) Supernova Digital Motion Art Festival. https://filmfreeway.com/Supernova.

Neither Paris Nor Sweden

Anon (1914) *[Gould can 5423.4].* Video online. http://archive.org/details/0633_Gould_can_5423_4_11_34_02_10.

Repeat Hikari

Baxter T and Canucci T (2018) *Conference exhibitions summer 2018.* https://vimeo.com/295693127/e95952e511.

Little Glass Men (2017) *Apache Force.* Free Music Archive. Music online. http://freemusicarchive.org/music/Little_Glass_Men/Future_Shapes/Apache_Force.

Supernova (2019) Supernova Digital Motion Art Festival. https://filmfreeway.com/Supernova.

Missing Kake Broek

The Conquering Light Of Flora And Fauna (2009) *Easy Christian Kill.* Free Music Archive. Music online. http://freemusicarchive.org/music/The_Conquering_Light_Of_Flora_And_Fauna/The_Hive/The_Conquering_Light_Of_Flora_And_Fauna_-_The_Hive_-_01_Easy_Christian_Kill.

OK, OK

Nine Inch Nails (2008) *1,000,000.* The Null Corporation. Music online. http://freemusicarchive.org/music/Nine_Inch_Nails/The_Slip/1000000.

Deliberare Humanum Est

Madame Rrose Sélavy (2014) *Despacho (Instrumental).* Free Music Archive. Music online. http://freemusicarchive.org/music/Madame_Rrose_Selavy/Bossa_Punk/Madame_Rrose_Slavy_-_Bossa_Punk_-_08_Despacho_Instrumental.

Chesapeake

BBC Sound Effects (2018) Cliff top with seagulls circling overhead (20C,reprocessed): 07046156.wav. http://bbcsfx.acropolis.org.uk/?q=cliff+top+with+seagulls+circling+overhead+(20c%2Creprocessed).

Blue Dot Sessions (2018) *Uncertain Ground.* Free Music Archive. Music online. http://freemusicarchive.org/music/Blue_Dot_Sessions/Duck_Lake/Uncertain_Ground.

Sound Living

BBC Sound Effects (2018) Church Bells: Single bell ringing, Notre Dame, Paris: 07030020.wav. http://bbcsfx.acropolis.org.uk/?q=church+bells+single+bell+ringing%2C+notre+dame%2C+paris.

BBC Sound Effects (2018) Seawash: Distant seawash and gulls (For use at low level): 07029145.wav. http://bbcsfx.acropolis.org.uk/?q=seawash+distant+seawash+and+gulls+(for+use+at+low+level).

Art Tartaruga

Blue Dot Sessions (2019) *Tartaruga.* Free Music Archive. Music online. http://freemusicarchive.org/music/Blue_Dot_Sessions/Orange_Cat/Tartaruga.

Menuetto Contained

Veesey D (2009) *Ludwig van Beethoven: Sonata No. 20 in G Major, Op. 49 No. 2, II. Tempo di menuetto.* MusOpen. Music online. https://freemusicarchive.org/music/Daniel_Veesey/Beethovens_Sonata_No_20_in_G_Major/Sonata_No_20_in_G_Major_Op_49_No_2_-_II_Tempo_di_menuetto.

Squares Circles and String

Jetson A (2018) *String Theory.* Free Music Archive. Music online.
https://freemusicarchive.org/music/Andre_Jetson.

Of Shui Mo Virtual

MacLeod K (2011) *Erik Satie: Gymnopedie No 2.* incompetech. Music online. https://
freemusicarchive.org/music/Kevin_MacLeod/Classical_Sampler/Gymnopedie_No_2.

Transmission is Ten

The Matt Kurz One (2012) *Wake up Little Siouxie.* Quote Unquoute. Music online.
https://freemusicarchive.org/music/The_Matt_Kurz_One/
IF_YOU_CANT_JOIN_EM_BEAT_EM/06_Wake_Up_Little_Siouxie.

isolation

Anderson D (2018) How Studio Ghibli cofounder Isao Takahata (1935–2018) breathed
melancholic grace into anime. *Frieze,* 10 April. https://frieze.com/article/how-studio-
ghibli-cofounder-isao-takahata-1935-2018-breathed-melancholic-grace-anime.

Blue Dot Sessions (2019) *I Recall.* Free Music Archive. Music online.
https://freemusicarchive.org/music/Blue_Dot_Sessions/RadioPink/I_Recall.

Flames Tear the Person

Beethoven L van (1802) Heiligenstädter Testament: ND VI 4281. Staats- und
Universitätsbibliothek Hamburg.
https://resolver.sub.uni-hamburg.de/kitodo/HANSw24716.

Czech National Symphony Orchestra (2020) *Ludwig van Beethoven: Symphony No. 3 in E Flat
Major Eroica, Op. 55 - II. Marcia funebre Adagio assai.* MusOpen. Music online.
https://musopen.org/music/2565-symphony-no-3-in-e-flat-major-eroica-op-55/.

Mills CW (1959) *The sociological imagination.* New York: Oxford University Press.

out of isolation came forth light

Denver Digitari (2020) Supernova 2020: World On Fire. Denver Digerati. Available at:
https://denverdigerati.org/world-on-fire.

M-PeX and feat. André Coelho (2017) *Luarne Raneficte.* Enough Records. Music online.
https://freemusicarchive.org/music/M-PeX/Carinae/07_m-pex_-
_luarne_raneficte__feat__andre_coelho.

M-PeX and feat. André Coelho (2017) *Navimort.* Enough Records. Music online.
https://freemusicarchive.org/music/M-PeX/Carinae/03_m-pex_-
_navimort__feat__andre_coelho.

Olma S (2016) *In defence of serendipity: for a radical politics of innovation.* London: Repeater.

Images on 'Additional links' pages. All are of Tizzy Canucci in locations in Second Life.
- Still image taken at *Sanctuary by the Sea* (p.37). This also formed a hand-crafted print edition entitled *Travelled all Night.*
- Image from the video art *Kite,* 2015 (p.38). https://vimeo.com/tizzycanucci/kite.
- Image from the video art *Repeat Hikari,* 2018 (p.39). Further detail on page 23.
- Still image taken at *Missing Melody* (this page).